COOKING THE GREEK WAY

This book is available in two editions:
Library binding by Lerner Publications Company,
    a division of Lerner Publishing Group
Soft cover by First Avenue Editions,
    an imprint of Lerner Publishing Group
241 First Avenue North
Minneapolis, MN 55401 U.S.A.

Website address: www.lernerbooks.com

Library of Congress Cataloging-in-Publication Data

Villos, Lynne W
       Cooking the Greek way / by Lynne W. Villos—Rev. & expanded
       p.   cm. — (Easy menu ethnic cookbooks)
    Includes index.
    ISBN: 0–8225–4131–9 (lib. bdg. : alk. paper)
    ISBN: 0–8225–0533–9 (pbk. : alk. paper)
       1. Cookery, Greek—Juvenile literature. 2. Greece—Social life and
       customs—Juvenile literature. [1. Cookery, Greek. 2. Greece—Social
    life and customs.] I. Title. II. Series.
    TX723.5.F8 V55 2002
    641.59495—DC 21   2001001804

Manufactured in the United States of America
1 2 3 4 5 6 – JR – 07 06 05 04 03 02

COOKING

revised and expanded

THE

to include new low-fat

GREEK

and vegetarian recipes

WAY

Lynne W. Villios

Lerner Publications Company • Minneapolis

Contents

Introduction

When one thinks of Greece, what often comes to mind is the ancient civilization that flourished there thousands of years ago. Ruins of this ancient culture still stand as reminders of Greece's glorious past. In modern times, Greece is an interesting combination of old and new. Even contemporary Greek cooking reflects ancient times, with dishes such as *dolmádes*, or stuffed grape leaves, dating back thousands of years.

Greece is located between western Europe and the Middle East, and Greek cooking combines influences from both of these regions. When the Romans invaded Greece in 197 B.C., for instance, they brought with them pasta and tomato sauce. Yogurt, rice, and many pastries came from the Persians, and coffee came from the Turks. These influences, along with those ingredients and methods that are uniquely Greek, created a cuisine that is both rich in tradition and extremely varied.

Stuffed grape leaves, or dolmádes, are a popular appetizer in Greece. Grape leaves are stuffed with a tasty blend of rice and ground lamb or beef. (Recipe on page 40.)

The Land

Greece is a land of sun and sea located in southeastern Europe. The country is surrounded on three sides by the sea: the Ionian Sea to the west, the Mediterranean Sea to the south, and the Aegean Sea to the east. A relatively small country, nearly one-quarter of Greece is made up of islands—437 in all—and can be divided into nine major land regions.

Macedonia-Thrace is a rocky, sparsely populated area in northeastern Greece. Tobacco is grown in the many valleys, and other crops are grown in the plains along the coast.

The Salonika Plain is Greece's most important agricultural area. Here, fruits, grains, and cotton are grown, and goats, sheep, and other livestock are raised. Sheep and goats graze in the Central Pindus region, a mountainous area where cotton, lemons, and olives are produced.

Thessaly is often called Greece's breadbasket because wheat is grown in abundance there. Fruits and olives are grown in Thessaly as well. Athens, the capital of Greece, is located in the Southeastern Uplands. Goats, wheat, and grapes are the major products of this area.

The Peloponnesus is a mountainous, rugged peninsula. Only about one-fourth of the land is used for growing crops, but some vegetables, grapes, olives, and grains are grown there. This area is most famous for its ancient ruins.

The Ionian Islands in the Ionian Sea produce many crops, including grains, olives, and grapes. Tobacco, grapes, barley, and wheat are the chief products of the Aegean Islands, and Crete, the largest Greek island, produces olives, grapes, sheep, and beef cattle.

The Food

Greece's climate and geography have always been major influences on its cuisine. The juicy lemons, tangy olives, fresh herbs, and vegetables that grow in Greece's warm sunshine are some of the country's best-loved foods.

Fishing is a major industry in Greece. The Mediterranean, Aegean, and Ionian Seas yield bountiful catches, and the Greeks enjoy many fish and seafood dishes, often flavored with oregano—the most popular Greek herb—and fresh lemon juice.

Greece's rocky, barren mountains are ideal for herds of goats and sheep, and these animals provide several important Greek foods.

Fishing boats dock in the harbor of the island of Mykonos.

Goat's milk is used both as a beverage and for making cheese, including tangy, white feta cheese, the best known of all Greek cheeses. This salty, crumbly cheese is eaten plain, used in salads, and added to stews and soups. Lamb is the most popular meat in Greece, although chicken, pork, and beef are enjoyed as well. Meat is often grilled over hot coals in outdoor pits. Olive trees grow all over in Greece, and the oil that is pressed from these olives is some of the finest in the world. In Greece, olive oil is used for frying, dressing salads, flavoring foods, and for making pastry dough. Greeks snack on cured olives and put them in salads.

Honey, which is found wild in all parts of Greece, is the Greeks' favorite sweetener and is used in many popular Greek pastries. Mount Hymettus near Athens is famous the world over for the wild honey found there.

Greek Cooking in Ancient Times

The art of cooking was appreciated thousands of years ago in ancient Greece. In fact, the world's first cookbook is said to have been written in 350 B.C. by the philosopher Archestratus. At that time, cooks were very highly regarded. They were not thought of as household help but as artists, and they were eagerly sought by employers.

The *Deipnosophistae,* or *Philosophy of Dining,* was written around A.D. 200 by a Greek man named Athenaeus. It presents a picture of the foods and eating customs of the ancient Greeks, including such famous authors as Sophocles and Homer. According to Athenaeus,

The ruins of the famous Parthenon temple are in Athens. Greece's capital city lies close to the sea, so fish is a big part of the local cuisine.

the ancient Greeks were the first to eat oysters, to grow cabbage and artichokes, and to create baked goods such as pastries and gingerbread.

The Greeks liked eating food that was very, very hot. In order not to burn their hands and fingers (spoons and forks were not yet invented), they trained themselves to withstand the hot temperatures by dipping their hands into hotter and hotter liquids every day.

Napkins were not invented until the fifteenth century, so the clothes of the ancient Greeks got very dirty at mealtime. Polite diners changed clothes between courses in order to appear clean and tidy.

The ancient Greeks had some other customs and beliefs that might seem odd in modern times. Grasshoppers were one of their greatest delicacies. They often served lettuce soup at the end of an evening meal because they thought it helped them sleep. Ancient Greeks also believed that honey could make them live longer. Democritus, a Greek who lived to be 109 years old, said the secret to his long life was eating honey and rubbing his skin with olive oil!

Holidays and Festivals

One can find a celebration almost every day of the year somewhere in Greece. Schools and businesses close on holidays, and people usually attend church. Nearly all Greeks belong to the Greek Orthodox Church, and most Greek holidays are religious. Whether it is one of the fourteen Greek Orthodox holidays, a name day, or a political holiday, a feast always accompanies the celebration.

Easter is the most important holiday in Greece. The Easter season begins with Carnival, about two months before Easter. Greeks celebrate Carnival with dancing, merrymaking, and parades with floats. On the last night of Carnival, people feast and dance throughout the night for the last time before the pre-Easter fasting of Lent begins.

On some holidays, Greeks dress in traditional costumes. Here, dancers celebrate the festival of Saint Paraskevi in the village of Metsovo.

Among other foods, they feast on tender spring lamb, macaroni and cheese, and eggs.

The serious, solemn period of Lent begins forty-eight days before Easter. During Lent, many Greeks do not eat meat, olive oil, fish, or dairy, and they do not drink wine. Clean Monday is the first day of Lent. Popular foods at this time are lentils and thick soups, breads made of flour and water, and vegetable dishes. Each day during Holy Week, the week leading up to Easter, the events of Christ's life are remembered. At exactly midnight at the Saturday night Easter church service, the priest announces that "Christ is risen." He holds a single lighted candle and lights candles held by the crowds.

After the midnight service, Greeks go home and feast on cakes and the traditional Easter soup, *mayeritsa*. This soup is made of the heart, liver, lungs, and intestines of a young lamb, along with dill, fennel, rice, lemons, and eggs. A Greek Easter custom is for each member of the family to hold an egg dyed deep red and press it against an egg held by someone else. The person whose egg breaks first is the winner. The deep-red eggs symbolize the blood of Christ, and the cracking of the eggs symbolizes the Resurrection (the rising of Christ from the dead).

The Easter Sunday feast is the big event of the year. Lamb flavored with herbs is roasted over hot coals, and braided bread decorated with the dyed eggs is served. Other foods included in a typical Easter feast are feta, olives, *taramosalata* (fish roe spread), Easter twists (pastries made with eggs, milk, and sesame seeds), spinach and feta salad, rice pilaf, artichokes à la Constantinople, shortbread cookies, and *baklavá* (honey and nut pastry).

Traditionally, Christmas in Greece was a strictly religious holiday rather than a time for presents. However, it has become more and more like Christmas in the United States, with Christmas trees and candles. Families reunite and enjoy a festive meal together. A traditional Christmas dinner might include cheese triangles, meat triangles, feta, pistachios, Christmas bread, country salad (endive, lettuce, olive, feta, tomato), roast suckling pig or stuffed turkey, whole cauliflower with artichokes, sweet potatoes, and *kourabiéthes* (sugar-coated butter cookies).

New Year's Day is also known as St. Basil's Day, named after the saint who answers wishes and brings gifts. On this day, the Greeks serve a special cake into which a silver coin is baked. Tradition says that whoever receives the piece of cake containing the coin will have good luck for the coming year. Another New Year's Day custom involves breaking open a pomegranate on the doorstep of the home. If the fruit has many seeds, the year will be happy and prosperous for the family. Greeks exchange gifts on New Year's Day rather than on Christmas. They also hold festive open-house parties, where guests are served appetizers, sweets, liquors, and coffee. For the New Year's Day feast, Greeks usually serve roast chicken, turkey, or lamb, rice pilaf, and many kinds of sweets including *melomakarouna* (honey cookies) and baklavá.

Greeks pay little attention to birthdays. Instead, people celebrate the day of the saint after whom they were named and they receive presents on that day. Villages, too, celebrate the day of their patron saint. The festivities often last for several days, with members of entire villages dancing and feasting together.

Before You Begin

Cooking any dish is easier and more fun if you are familiar with its ingredients. Greek cooking makes use of some ingredients that you may not know. Sometimes special cookware is used, too, although the recipes in this book can easily be prepared with ordinary utensils and pans.

The most important thing you need to know before you start is how to be a careful cook. On the following page, you'll find a few rules that will make your cooking experience safe, fun, and easy. Next, take a look at the "dictionary" of utensils, terms, and special ingredients. You may also want to read the list of tips on preparing healthy, low-fat meals.

When you've picked out a recipe to try, read through it from beginning to end. Then you are ready to shop for ingredients and to organize the cookware you will need. Once you have assembled everything, you're ready to begin cooking.

Vasilopeta, or New Year's bread, is traditionally baked on New Year's Eve. A coin baked inside brings good luck to the person who finds it. (Recipe on page 68.)

The Careful Cook

Whenever you cook, there are certain safety rules you must always keep in mind. Even experienced cooks follow these rules when they are in the kitchen.

- Always wash your hands before handling food. Thoroughly wash all raw vegetables and fruits to remove dirt, chemicals, and insecticides. Wash uncooked poultry, fish, and meat under cold water.
- Use a cutting board when cutting up vegetables and fruits. Don't cut them up in your hand! And be sure to cut in a direction *away* from you and your fingers.
- Long hair or loose clothing can easily catch fire if brought near the burners of a stove. If you have long hair, tie it back before you start cooking.
- Turn all pot handles toward the back of the stove so that you will not catch your sleeves or jewelry on them. This is especially important when younger brothers and sisters are around. They could easily knock off a pot and get burned.
- Always use a pot holder to steady hot pots or to take pans out of the oven. Don't use a wet cloth on a hot pan because the steam it produces could burn you.
- Lift the lid of a steaming pot with the opening away from you so that you will not get burned.
- If you get burned, hold the burn under cold running water. Do not put grease or butter on it. Cold water helps to take the heat out, but grease or butter will only keep it in.
- If grease or cooking oil catches fire, throw baking soda or salt at the bottom of the flame to put it out. (Water will *not* put out a grease fire.) Call for help, and try to turn all the stove burners to "off."

Cooking Utensils

colander—A bowl-shaped dish with holes in it that is used for washing or draining food

Dutch oven—A heavy pot with a tight-fitting domed cover that is often used for cooking soups or stews

pastry brush—A small brush with nylon bristles used for coating food with melted butter or other liquid

skewer—A thin metal rod used to hold small pieces of meat or vegetables for broiling or grilling

spatula—A flat, thin utensil, usually metal or plastic, used to lift, toss, turn, or scoop up food

whisk—A small wire utensil used for beating ingredients by hand

Cooking Terms

baste—To pour, brush, or spoon liquid over food as it roasts in order to flavor and moisten it

boil—To heat a liquid over high heat until bubbles form and rise rapidly to the surface

broil—To cook directly under a heat source so that the side of the food facing the heat cooks rapidly

brown—To cook food quickly in fat over high heat so that the surface turns an even brown

dash—A small amount; a quick shake or sprinkle

fold—To blend an ingredient with other ingredients by using a gentle overturning circular motion instead of by stirring or beating

garnish—To decorate with small pieces of food such as parsley sprigs

grate—To cut food into tiny pieces by rubbing it against a grater

marinate—To soak food in a liquid, which adds flavor and tenderizes it mince—To chop food into very small pieces

preheat—To allow an oven to warm up to a certain temperature before putting food in it

roast—To cook in an open pan in an oven so that heat penetrates the food from all sides

sauté—To fry quickly over high heat in oil or fat, stirring or turning the food to prevent burning

simmer—To cook over low heat in liquid kept just below its boiling point. Bubbles may occasionally rise to the surface.

Special Ingredients

almond extract—A liquid made from the oil of the almond nut and used to give an almond flavor to food

bay leaf—The dried leaf of the bay (also called laurel) tree. It is used to season food.

currants—Small, dried, seedless grapes similar to raisins

dill—An herb whose seeds and leaves are both used in cooking. Dried dill is called dill weed.

feta cheese—Crumbly, white cheese made from goat or sheep milk

grape leaves—The leaves of grapevine plants, usually found packed in jars with brine (salt water) and used in many Greek recipes as wrappers for various fillings. Grape leaves are available at many supermarkets and at specialty stores.

greek olives—Black olives, usually pickled in brine, with wrinkled skin and a slightly tart taste

kefalotiri cheese—Greek grating cheese

lentils—The flat, edible seeds of the lentil plant

marjoram—A fragrant herb of the mint family often used in Greek cooking

olive oil—An oil made by pressing olives. It is used in cooking and for dressing salads.

orzo—A small, rice-shaped pasta

phyllo—Paper-thin dough used in many Greek recipes. Phyllo is available frozen at many supermarkets and at specialty stores.

pine nuts—The edible seed of certain pine trees. Pine nuts can be expensive, but chopped almonds or walnuts are good substitutes.

red-wine vinegar—A vinegar made with red wine that is often used with oil for dressing salads

ricotta cheese—A white cheese made with whole or skim milk that resembles cottage cheese

scallions—A variety of green onion

slivered almonds—Almonds that have been split into thin strips

Working with Phyllo

Phyllo dough is paper-thin dough made of flour and water. It is used with various fillings for many Greek dishes. Phyllo dough is available frozen in many supermarkets and in specialty stores. Each sheet is brushed well with melted butter before baking. This makes the phyllo turn light, flaky, golden, and delicious. Phyllo is extremely fragile, but using it is not difficult if you follow these basic rules:

1. Thaw frozen phyllo in its original package for 24 hours in the refrigerator.
2. Do not unwrap phyllo until you are ready to use it. Make sure your work area is cleared, your melted butter and pastry brush are ready, and your filling is prepared.
3. Remove rings from your fingers and make sure your fingernails are not too long. (Fingernails can tear the phyllo.)
4. Work with one sheet at a time. Peel sheets carefully from package.
5. After removing a sheet, cover remaining sheets tightly with either plastic wrap or a slightly damp kitchen towel (not terry cloth).
6. Leftover phyllo will stay fresh in the refrigerator for one week if covered well with plastic wrap.
7. If phyllo is not available where you live, you can substitute frozen puff pastry, thawed and rolled very thin with a rolling pin. It won't be as thin as phyllo, so use one or two fewer layers than called for in a recipe.

How to Stuff a Grape Leaf

1. Place a grape leaf shiny side down on a plate or countertop, making sure leaf is flat.
2. Place 1 teaspoon of filling in the center of the leaf.
3. Fold stem end over filling.
4. Fold each side of leaf, one at a time, over filling, enclosing filling completely.
5. Roll up leaf from stem end toward the tip until you have a small, compact roll. Gently squeeze roll in the palm of your hand to seal edges.
6. Use rice fillings sparingly, and do not wrap grape leaves too tightly, as rice will expand when cooked.

Healthy and Low-Fat Cooking Tips

Many modern cooks are concerned about preparing healthy, low-fat meals. Fortunately, there are simple ways to reduce the fat content of most dishes. Here are a few general tips for adapting the recipes in this book. Throughout the book, you'll also find specific suggestions for individual recipes—and don't worry, they'll still taste delicious!

Many recipes call for butter or oil to sauté vegetables or other ingredients. Using oil lowers saturated fat right away. Greek recipes call for large amounts of oil, so you can also reduce the amount of oil you use. You can also substitute a low-fat or nonfat cooking spray for oil. Sprinkling a little salt on tvegetables brings out their natural juices, so less oil is needed. It's also a good idea to use a small, non-stick frying pan if you decide to use less oil than the recipe calls for.

Another common substitution for butter is margarine. Before making this substitution, consider the recipe. If it is a dessert, it's often best to use butter, and if you are working with phyllo, it is best to use butter or oil. Margarine may noticeably change the taste or consistency of the food.

Cheese is a common source of unwanted fat. Many cheeses are available in reduced or nonfat varieties, but keep in mind that these varieties often don't melt as well. Another easy way to reduce the amount of fat from cheese is simply to use less of it! To avoid losing flavor, you might try using a stronger-tasting cheese. Many Greek recipes call for feta cheese. Most American-made feta is lower in fat than other cheeses such as cheddar, provolone, Swiss, or Muenster.

Some cooks like to replace ground beef with ground turkey to lower fat. However, since this does change the flavor, you may need to experiment a little bit to decide if you like this substitution. Buying extra-lean ground beef is also an easy way to reduce fat.

A way to make your desserts healthier is to reduce their sugar content. Experiment by taking out more and more sugar each time you make the recipe. You'll be surprised to find out that desserts can still taste great!

There are many ways to prepare meals that are good for you and still taste great. As you become a more experienced cook, try experimenting with recipes and substitutions to find the methods that work best for you.

METRIC CONVERSIONS

Cooks in the United States measure both liquid and solid ingredients using standard containers based on the 8-ounce cup and the tablespoon. These measurements are based on volume, while the metric system of measurement is based on both weight (for solids) and volume (for liquids). To convert from U.S. fluid tablespoons, ounces, quarts, and so forth to metric liters is a straightforward conversion, using the chart below. However, since solids have different weights—one cup of rice does not weigh the same as one cup of grated cheese, for example—many cooks who use the metric system have kitchen scales to weigh different ingredients. The chart below will give you a good starting point for basic conversions to the metric system.

MASS (weight)

1 ounce (oz.)	=	28.0 grams (g)
8 ounces	=	227.0 grams
1 pound (lb.) or 16 ounces	=	0.45 kilograms (kg)
2.2 pounds	=	1.0 kilogram

LIQUID VOLUME

1 teaspoon (tsp.)	=	5.0 milliliters (ml)
1 tablespoon (tbsp.)	=	15.0 milliliters
1 fluid ounce (oz.)	=	30.0 milliliters
1 cup (c.)	=	240 milliliters
1 pint (pt.)	=	480 milliliters
1 quart (qt.)	=	0.95 liters (l)
1 gallon (gal.)	=	3.80 liters

LENGTH

¼ inch (in.)	=	0.6 centimeters (cm)
½ inch	=	1.25 centimeters
1 inch	=	2.5 centimeters

TEMPERATURE

212°F	=	100°C (boiling point of water)
225°F	=	110°C
250°F	=	120°C
275°F	=	135°C
300°F	=	150°C
325°F	=	160°C
350°F	=	180°C
375°F	=	190°C
400°F	=	200°C

(To convert temperature in Fahrenheit to Celsius, subtract 32 and multiply by .56)

PAN SIZES

8-inch cake pan	=	20 x 4-centimeter cake pan
9-inch cake pan	=	23 x 3.5-centimeter cake pan
11 x 7-inch baking pan	=	28 x 18-centimeter baking pan
13 x 9-inch baking pan	=	32.5 x 23-centimeter baking pan
9 x 5-inch loaf pan	=	23 x 13-centimeter loaf pan
2-quart casserole	=	2-liter casserole

A Greek Table

The Greeks are known for their hospitality and love of entertaining. A Greek would never think not to offer a visitor something to eat or drink, and it would be considered just as rude for a visitor to refuse the offer. One tradition is to offer a guest a *glyko*, or "spoon sweet," which is a thick jam of fruits or vegetables such as peach, quince, apricot, tomato, or eggplant. The glyko is served on a tray with a glass of ice water and a cup of thick, sweet Greek coffee. Offering these treats welcomes the visitor and shows the family's happiness at having a guest.

Whether it's outside or indoors, Greek families dine together.

A Greek Menu

Family ties and traditions are very important to the Greeks. In the cities, lunch is a light meal. There, the whole family comes together for the evening meal, which is usually eaten at about 10 P.M. In rural areas, however, lunch is the main meal of the day. Everyday family meals are generally very simple. You can prepare authentic and delicious Greek meals for your own family and friends. Make the meal a festive occasion, as the Greeks do, by enjoying lively conversation along with the flavorful foods. As the Greeks would say, *"Kali orexi!"* (Happy eating!). Below are menus for two sample meals, along with shopping lists of necessary ingredients to prepare these meals.

MEAL 1

Skewered lamb

Orzo with browned butter sauce

Greek salad

Honey cheese pie

SHOPPING LIST:

Produce

1 head lettuce
2 tomatoes
1 cucumber
1 green pepper
5 scallions
3 lemons
garlic

Dairy/Egg/Meat

2 lb. lamb
6 oz. feta cheese
3 tbsp. Parmesan cheese
2 c. ricotta cheese
4 eggs
⅓ c. butter

Canned/Bottled/Boxed

olive oil
black olives
red-wine vinegar
1 c. honey
½ lb. orzo
all-purpose flour

Miscellaneous

salt
pepper
marjoram
oregano
cinnamon

MEAL 2

Egg and lemon soup

Spinach pie

Cucumber and yogurt dip

Chocolate bells

SHOPPING LIST:

Produce

1 clove garlic
2 lb. fresh spinach
1 bunch scallions
½ c. parsley
2½ tbsp. dill weed
2 lemons
1 medium cucumber

Dairy/Egg/Meat

6 eggs
6 oz. feta cheese
¾ c. butter
4 tbsp. cream
1 c. plain, lowfat yogurt

Canned/Bottled/Boxed

½ lb. (about 14 sheets) phyllo
3 10½-oz. cans chicken broth
½ c. rice
3¼ c. powdered sugar
rum flavoring
olive oil
white vinegar

Miscellaneous

salt
pepper
nutmeg
1 lb. shelled walnuts or pecans
1 lb. sweet milk chocolate

29

Lunch / Yéfma

In the rural parts of Greece, the midday meal is often eaten at around 1:00 or 2:00 P.M. In the cities, lunch is a rather light meal, much like lunch in the United States. In the countryside, it is the main meal of the day. After this large lunch, schools and businesses close, and people stay at home for an afternoon rest, a custom similar to the Spanish and Mexican *siesta*. Even during these quiet hours after lunch, the Greeks love to snack, and they munch on cookies and other sweets with their coffee.

This delicious spinach pie, or spanikópita, is made with feta cheese, scallions, and dill and is baked inside a flaky crust of phyllo. (Recipe on page 34.)

Skewered Lamb/ Arní Souvlákia

Souvlákia is especially good when cooked the Greek way—on an outdoor grill—but is also delicious when broiled in the oven. You can vary this souvlákia recipe by alternating pieces of marinated meat with chunks of green pepper, onion, and tomato. Leg of lamb is best for souvlákia, but you can also use beef or chicken. For a vegetarian dish, skip the meat altogether and marinate fresh vegetables instead.

2 tbsp. olive oil

3 tbsp. lemon juice

½ tsp. salt

⅛ tsp. pepper

½ tsp. marjoram

2 lb. lamb, cut into 2-inch cubes

1 lemon, cut into wedges

*Inexpensive metal skewers are available at most grocery stores.

1. Mix all ingredients except lamb and lemons in a large, flat dish.

2. Add lamb and stir to coat pieces well. Cover the dish with plastic wrap and let stand in refrigerator for at least 30 minutes.

3. Spear the cubes of meat onto 4 long metal skewers.* Place skewers in a shallow broiling pan.

4. Place oven rack about 6 inches from top heat source. Turn on oven to broil.

5. Broil meat for 10 minutes. Then turn over the skewers and broil 10 minutes more.

6. Holding skewers with a pot holder, remove lamb with a fork and serve with lemon wedges.

Preparation time: 25 minutes
Cooking and marination time: 50 minutes
Serves 4

Spinach Pie/ *Spanikópita*

Spanikópita, or spinach pie, is one of the most famous Greek dishes. It is made with phyllo pastry, which is paper-thin dough sold either fresh or frozen. See page 22 for tips on handling this delicious dough. Spanikópita can be served hot as a main or side dish, or cold as a snack or appetizer.

2 lb. fresh spinach (or 2 10-oz. packages frozen chopped spinach, thawed)

¼ c. olive oil

½ c. chopped scallions

¼ c. finely chopped fresh parsley

2 tbsp. finely chopped fresh dill, or 1 tbsp. dried dill weed

4 eggs, lightly beaten

1 c. (about 6 oz.) finely crumbled feta cheese

½ tsp. salt

¼ tsp. pepper

dash of nutmeg

¾ c. (1½ sticks) butter*, melted

½ lb. (about 14 sheets) phyllo pastry, thawed

1. Preheat oven to 350°F.

2. Remove large, tough stems from spinach leaves. Wash spinach leaves in cold water to remove all dirt and sand. Using your hands, squeeze water from spinach and dry on paper towels.

3. Chop spinach into ¼-inch pieces. (If using frozen spinach, place thawed spinach in a colander and squeeze out excess moisture by pressing spinach with the back of a large spoon.)

4. Heat olive oil in a large frying pan over medium-high heat. Add scallions and cook 4 minutes, stirring constantly. Add spinach and cook 3 more minutes.

5. Remove pan from heat and let cool for 5 minutes.

6. Stir in parsley, dill, eggs, feta cheese, salt, pepper, and nutmeg and set aside.

7. Butter a 9×13-inch baking pan. Place 1 sheet of phyllo pastry in pan. Brush sheet well with melted butter, then put another sheet on top of it. Continue adding sheets, brushing each one with butter, until there are a total of 7 sheets.

8. Spread spinach filling evenly over phyllo. Trim off dried edges of phyllo with scissors or sharp knife. Then fold excess phyllo over the filling.

9. Place 7 sheets of phyllo pastry over the spinach, one at a time, brushing each sheet well with melted butter before adding the next.

10. Trim off excess phyllo with a pair of scissors or a sharp knife. Brush top of pie with melted butter.

11. Place pan on middle oven rack and bake 40 minutes or until crust is golden. Cool 5 minutes before cutting into squares.

For a meal that is lower in saturated fat, try substituting some olive oil for the butter.

Preparation time: 30 minutes
Cooking and assembly time: 1 hour 45 minutes
Serves 8 to 12

Greek Salad/ Salάta

Greeks always serve a salad with meals. The following recipe is the classic Greek salad featuring feta cheese.

½ head iceberg or romaine lettuce

2 tomatoes, quartered, or 10 cherry tomatoes, cut in half

1 cucumber, peeled and sliced

½ green pepper, cored, seeded, and cut into strips

5 scallions, thinly sliced

1 c. (about 6 oz.) feta cheese, broken into chunks

12 to 16 black Greek olives

1. Tear lettuce into bite-sized pieces and place in a large salad bowl.

2. Add tomatoes, cucumber, green pepper, scallions, feta cheese, and olives.

3. Pour dressing (recipe follows) over salad and toss.

4. Serve on chilled salad plates.

Dressing:

2 tbsp. red-wine vinegar

1 clove garlic, finely chopped

¼ tsp. salt

⅛ tsp. pepper

½ tsp. oregano

⅓ c. olive oil*

1. Whisk together all ingredients except olive oil.

2. Slowly add the olive oil, whisking constantly.

Preparation time: 30 minutes
Serves 4

*Use less olive oil for a dressing
that is lower in fat.

Appetizers / Mezéthes

In the early evening, after their afternoon rest, many Greek people ward off their predinner hunger by stopping by a taverna, which is a family-run café, for refreshments. At Greek tavernas, people sit, chat, and play a popular game called backgammon with friends while sipping beverages and nibbling on *mezethes*, or appetizers. These include olives, chunks of feta cheese, fried eggplant, greens in olive oil and lemon sauce, bread, and dips. These mezethes, along with soups, are also often served as the first course of a large meal.

Whether it's a midafternoon snack or part of a larger meal, lentil soup, or faki, and cucumber and yogurt dip, or tzatzíki, tantalize the taste buds. (Recipes on pages 44 and 45.)

Stuffed Grape Leaves/*Dolmádes*

Stuffed grape leaves are one of Greece's most famous—and most ancient—foods. Grape leaves can be purchased in jars at many supermarkets and specialty stores. They are packed in brine (or salt water) and must be rinsed thoroughly before using. You may want to ask a friend to help you fill and roll up the grape leaves.

2 c. cooked white rice

1 lb. ground lamb or ground beef*

½ c. finely chopped scallions

¼ c. currants

¼ c. pine nuts or chopped almonds

2 tbsp. fresh mint, chopped (optional)

½ tsp. salt

2 tbsp. finely chopped fresh parsley

2 tbsp. olive oil

1 1-lb. jar grape leaves

¼ c. lemon juice

1 10½-oz. can beef broth

1 c. water

3 lemons, cut into wedges

1. Cook rice according to directions on package.

2. Place lamb or beef in a large skillet. Cook meat over medium-high heat until brown, stirring to break up into small pieces.

3. Remove meat from heat. Drain off fat and set aside.

4. In a large bowl, combine cooked rice, meat, scallions, currants, nuts, mint, salt, parsley, and olive oil. Stir gently with a spoon.

5. Drain grape leaves in a colander. Carefully rinse the grape leaves in cool running water. Drain on paper towels. Use a sharp knife to cut stems off leaves.

6. Place 1 tsp. meat mixture on a grape leaf and fold (as described on page 23). Repeat until all filling is used.

7. In a large saucepan, arrange the rolls in layers, seam-side down. Sprinkle 1 tbsp. of lemon juice over each layer.

8. Pour any remaining lemon juice, the beef broth, and the water over the dolmádes.

9. Place a heavy plate or baking dish on top of the dolmádes to hold them in place while cooking. Cover saucepan and cook over low heat for 1 hour.

10. Remove from heat and allow to cool. Carefully remove the plate and drain off all cooking liquid.

11. Serve cold or at room temperature with lemon wedges.

*For a vegetarian option, use another cup of cooked rice and double the amount of nuts and currants in place of the meat. Use vegetable broth instead of beef broth.

Preparation time: 35 minutes
Cooking and assembly time: 3 hours
Makes about 40 to 50 dolmádes

Egg and Lemon Soup/Soúpa Avgolémono

Delicate egg and lemon soup is probably the number-one soup in Greece. Be careful to add the hot broth slowly to the eggs, beating all the while. The extra effort will be well worth it!

3 10½-oz. cans (about 4 c.) chicken broth

⅓ c. rice, uncooked

2 eggs

4 tbsp. lemon juice

4 thin slices lemon for garnish

2 tsp. chopped fresh parsley for garnish

*For a creamy variation, add ½ c. heavy cream after step 2.

1. In a heavy saucepan, bring chicken broth to a boil. Turn down heat. Add rice and stir.

2. Cover pan and simmer 12 to 15 minutes or until rice is tender.*

3. While rice is cooking, beat eggs and lemon juice together with a wire whisk. Set aside.

4. When rice is cooked, remove pan from heat.

5. Carefully add 2 c. hot broth to the egg-lemon mixture, a little at a time, whisking constantly. (If you add the broth too quickly or don't keep whisking, the eggs will curdle.)

6. Add the egg mixture to the remaining broth and rice and whisk together.

7. Serve in soup bowls with a thin slice of lemon and a sprinkle of chopped fresh parsley floating on top.

Preparation time: 10 minutes
Cooking time: 20 minutes
Serves 4

Lentil Soup/*Fakí*

In Greece, *fakí* is traditionally eaten on Good Friday (the Friday before Easter). The Greek Orthodox Church prohibits eating meat or fish on that day, and lentil soup is a nourishing alternative.

1 lb. lentils

3 tbsp. olive oil

1 medium onion, finely chopped

1 stalk celery, finely chopped

2 carrots, peeled and cut into
⅛-inch-thick slices

2 cloves garlic, finely chopped

1 bay leaf

¼ tsp. pepper

1 tsp. oregano

2 tbsp. tomato paste

8 c. cold water

1 tsp. salt

½ c. red-wine vinegar*

½ c. chopped fresh parsley

1. Spread lentils evenly on a cookie sheet. Pick out any small stones or other foreign objects. Place lentils in a colander and rinse thoroughly with cold water.

2. Heat oil in a large kettle over medium-high heat. Add onions, celery, and carrots and sauté for 5 minutes.

3. Add lentils, garlic, bay leaf, pepper, oregano, tomato paste, and 8 c. cold water, or enough to cover. Bring to a boil.

4. Cover kettle and simmer over low heat for 1 hour. (You may need to add more water if soup becomes too thick.)

5. Add salt and vinegar to lentil mixture and stir well. Cover and simmer, stirring occasionally, for 30 minutes more, or until lentils are tender.

6. Stir in parsley and serve in individual soup bowls.

*For a tangier flavor, you can substitute lemon juice for the vinegar.

Preparation time: 30 minutes
Cooking time: 2 hours
Serves 6 to 8

Cucumber and Yogurt Dip / Tzatziki

Cucumbers were brought to Greece from Asia centuries ago, and yogurt's origins are in the Middle East. The Greeks combine them in this refreshing meze (appetizer), which is especially good on a hot day.

1 medium cucumber

1 clove garlic, finely chopped

3 scallions, finely chopped

1 tsp. olive oil

½ tsp. white vinegar

1 tsp. finely chopped fresh dill or ½ tsp. dried dill weed

1 c. (8 oz.) plain, lowfat or nonfat yogurt

1. Peel cucumber. Cut in half lengthwise and scoop out and discard seeds. Cut into small chunks to make about 1 c.

2. In a small bowl, mix cucumber with garlic, scallions, olive oil, vinegar, and dill.

3. Add yogurt and stir gently to combine.

4. Cover and chill 2 hours or more.

5. Serve as a salad on lettuce leaves garnished with tomato slices or as a dip with bread and raw vegetables.

Preparation time: 20 minutes
Refrigeration time: 2 hours
Makes about 1½ c.

Dinner / Déipnon

In Greece, as in many other European countries, dinner is eaten rather late—often not until 10 P.M. At this time, the family comes together for an appetizer, salad, a meat or fish dish, vegetables, potatoes, rice or pasta, and wine. It is common for Greeks to sit in their dining room or at a restaurant until midnight or even later. In the country, where lunch is the main meal of the day, people eat a smaller dinner, perhaps only a salad, cheese, and bread. Whether you serve the following Greek specialties at noon or in the evening, they are sure to satisfy anyone's appetite.

Hearty beef and onion stew, or stifádo, and orzo with browned butter sauce make a filling meal. (Recipes on pages 50 and 51.)

Baked Fish / Psári Plakí

Since Greece is surrounded by the sea on three sides, Greeks eat many delicious fish and seafood dishes. For psári plakí, cod, haddock, or bluefish fillets work well. If you use frozen fillets, thaw them completely before preparing this dish.

2 tbsp. olive oil

2 lb. fish fillets

½ tsp. salt

¼ tsp. pepper

2 tbsp. lemon juice

1 medium onion, thinly sliced

¼ c. finely chopped fresh parsley

1 8-oz. can diced tomatoes

1. Preheat oven to 350°F.

2. Brush a 9×13-inch baking dish with olive oil. Place fish in baking dish. Sprinkle with salt, pepper, and lemon juice.

3. Place onion slices on top of fish and sprinkle parsley over all.

4. Drain tomatoes and scatter over fish, onions, and parsley.*

5. Place baking dish on middle oven rack and bake 30 minutes, or until tender, basting occasionally with pan juices.

Preparation time: 25 minutes
Cooking time: 30 minutes
Serves 4

*For a variation, try adding sautéed chopped scallions, celery, and carrots with the tomatoes to the fish before baking.

Beef and Onion Stew / Stifádo

Stifádo is a hearty stew that is especially good in cool weather.

3 tbsp. vegetable oil

2 lb. beef chuck or top round, cut into 2-inch cubes

3 c. thinly sliced onions

2 cloves garlic, finely chopped

1 6-oz. can tomato paste

1 10½-oz. can beef broth

1 c. water

¼ c. red-wine vinegar

½ tsp. salt

⅛ tsp. pepper

¼ tsp. cinnamon

1 bay leaf

To vary this savory dish, add 1 c. finely crumbled feta cheese before serving.

1. In a Dutch oven, heat oil over medium-high heat until it begins to sizzle.

2. Add meat and brown on all sides. When browned, carefully remove meat with a spatula or a slotted spoon and set aside.

3. Put onions and garlic in the Dutch oven and cook until lightly browned.

4. Return meat to the Dutch oven. Add tomato paste, beef broth, water, vinegar, salt, pepper, cinnamon, and bay leaf. Mix well.

5. Cover Dutch oven and turn heat to low. Simmer stew about 3 to 4 hours, or until the meat is very tender. Stir every 15 minutes to prevent meat from sticking to the Dutch oven. The sauce will become very thick, almost like jam.

6. Remove bay leaf and serve.*

Preparation time: 30 minutes
Cooking time: 3½ to 4½ hours
Serves 4 to 6

Orzo with Browned Butter Sauce/
Orzo Kauto Voutyro

Orzo is a rice-shaped pasta available at most supermarkets and co-ops. If you can't get orzo, you can substitute any small pasta or white rice.

½ lb. orzo, uncooked

⅓ c. butter or margarine

3 tbsp. grated Parmesan cheese*

1. Cook orzo according to directions on package. Drain in a colander and set aside.

2. While orzo is cooking, put butter in a small saucepan. Melt over medium-high heat and cook until butter turns brown.

3. Place hot, drained orzo in a serving bowl. Pour butter and Parmesan cheese over orzo and stir to combine. Serve immediately.

Preparation time: 5 minutes
Cooking time: 20 minutes
Serves 4

For extra zip, substitute kefalotiri cheese for the Parmesan cheese.

Stuffed Tomatoes with Feta Cheese/
Domátes mé Féta

For this recipe, it is important to use the reddest, ripest tomatoes available. If your tomatoes aren't quite ripe (pinkish-orange instead of bright red), place them in a brown paper bag and keep in a cupboard or other dark place for a day or two to ripen.

4 medium-sized ripe tomatoes

2 tbsp. finely chopped scallions

2 tbsp. finely chopped fresh parsley

½ c. (about 3 oz.) finely crumbled feta cheese

¼ c. bread crumbs

3 tbsp. olive oil

1. Preheat oven to 350°F.

2. Carefully cut tops off tomatoes. Using a spoon, carefully scoop out pulp and seeds. Save pulp and discard seeds.

3. Coarsely chop the tomato pulp.

4. In a small bowl, combine tomato pulp with scallions, parsley, feta cheese, bread crumbs, and olive oil.

5. Spoon mixture into the hollowed-out tomatoes. Place tomatoes right side up in an 8×8-inch baking pan and bake 15 minutes.

6. Serve stuffed tomatoes steaming hot.

Preparation time: 30 minutes
Cooking time: 15 minutes
Serves 4

Dessert/Disert

The Greek people love sweets of all kinds, including puddings, cakes, and ice creams. It is obvious when looking in any *zacharoplasteio* (pastry shop) window that Greeks are master dessert makers. Greeks tend to eat desserts in the late afternoon with hot coffee or, in the summer, with iced coffee. Most Greeks also end their meals with a simple dessert of cold fresh fruit, such as watermelon, or with fresh yogurt. You may want to top off your Greek feasts with one of the following recipes. You and your family will no doubt enjoy any of these delectable Greek treats.

Baklavá is perhaps the most famous of Greek desserts. The pastry is made with walnuts, honey, and phyllo. (Recipe on page 60.)

Butter Cookies/ *Kourabiethes*

Butter cookies are very popular year-round in Greece. At Christmastime, they are topped with whole cloves to symbolize the spices brought to the baby Jesus by the Wise Men.

2½ c. all-purpose flour

I teaspooon baking powder

¼ tsp. salt

I c. (2 sticks) butter, softened

½ c. sugar

I egg

½ tsp. vanilla extract

¼ tsp. almond extract

powdered sugar for sprinkling

*For a variation, add ½ c. chopped blanched almonds to the soft dough.

1. Preheat oven to 350°F.

2. In a small bowl, combine flour, baking powder, and salt.

3. In a large bowl, beat together butter, sugar, and egg until light and fluffy. Add flour mixture to butter mixture and mix until well blended. Add vanilla and almond extracts and mix well.*

4. With your hands, form dough into balls, crescents, or S-shapes, using about ½ tbsp. at a time.

5. Place cookies 2 inches apart on a cookie sheet. Put cookie sheet on middle oven rack and bake 15 minutes, or until barely brown around the edges.

6. Remove cookies from cookie sheet with spatula and cool on wire rack for 5 minutes.

7. With a flour sifter, sprinkle powdered sugar over cookies.

Preparation time: 35 minutes
Cooking time: 15 minutes
Makes about 3 dozen cookies

Honey Cheese Pie/Melópitta

4 eggs

2 c. (16 oz.) ricotta cheese

1 c. honey

½ tsp. cinnamon

2 tbsp. all-purpose flour

1 tsp. lemon juice*

1 tbsp. butter

cinnamon for sprinkling

1. Preheat oven to 350°F.

2. Beat eggs lightly in a large mixing bowl.

3. Add ricotta cheese, honey, cinnamon, flour, and lemon juice. Beat for 3 minutes, or until very smooth.

4. Rub 1 tbsp. butter into a 9-inch pie pan, then pour in pie mixture.

5. Place pan on middle oven rack and bake 1 hour, or until the surface of the pie cracks and is puffed.

6. Remove pie from oven and sprinkle with cinnamon.

7. Cool to room temperature before cutting into wedges to serve.

Preparation time: 20 minutes
Cooking time: 1 hour
Serves 8 to 10

For a tangier flavor, add another tablespoon of lemon juice.

Walnut-Honey Pastry/*Baklavā*

Baklavá is a sweet pastry made with phyllo dough, so read over the instructions on page 22 for tips on working with the fragile phyllo sheets.

Syrup ingredients:

1 c. sugar*

1 c. water

1½-inch-thick slice lemon

1 stick cinnamon

1 c. honey

1. In a small saucepan, combine sugar, water, lemon, and cinnamon.

2. Bring to a boil over medium heat. Reduce heat and simmer 10 minutes.

3. Remove pan from heat. Stir in honey and cool well. When cool, remove the lemon and cinnamon.

Pastry ingredients:

4 c. (1 lb.) finely ground walnuts

2 c. (½ lb.) finely ground blanched or unblanched almonds

¼ c. sugar

2 tsp. cinnamon

½ tsp. nutmeg

1½ c. (3 sticks) butter, melted

1 1-lb. package phyllo dough, thawed

1. Preheat oven to 300°F.

2. In a large bowl, combine walnuts, almonds, sugar, cinnamon, and nutmeg.

3. Butter a 9×13-inch pan with 2 tbsp. butter. Place 4 sheets of phyllo in the pan, brushing each with melted butter before adding the next. Butter the fourth sheet also.

4. Sprinkle ½ to ¾ c. of nut mixture over the phyllo. Top nut mixture with 2 more sheets of phyllo, buttering each sheet well.

5. Continue alternating nut mixture with 2 sheets buttered phyllo until both are used up, ending with phyllo. Brush top with butter.

6. With a sharp knife, trim off any excess phyllo on the sides of the pastry.

7. With a sharp knife, cut 1½-inch-wide lengthwise strips in the dough. (Do not cut all the way through the dough. Cut through the top layer only.)

8. Make 1½-inch diagonal cuts to create diamond-shaped pieces. (Cut through the top layer only.)

9. Bake for 1 hour, or until golden brown. Remove from oven and place on a cooling rack.

10. Cut through diamonds completely with a sharp knife. Immediately pour the cooled syrup over hot pastry.

11. Cool and serve on dessert plates.

If you prefer a baklavá that is less sweet, reduce the amount of sugar by half.

Preparation time: 1 hour 30 minutes
Cooking time: 1 hour 15 minutes
Makes about 3 dozen pieces

Holiday and Festival Food

Holidays are occasions for fun with family and friends, and no Greek holiday or festival would be complete without a feast. Greeks serve a variety of soups and breads at almost all holiday celebrations. Christmas, Easter, and New Year's each have a special, delicious bread, full of eggs and sweet butter. Greeks eat all kinds of mouthwatering sweets, such as cookies, cakes, and pastries during their celebrations. Following are a few of the many traditional Greek holiday and festival recipes.

Holiday meat pie and dyed Easter eggs are among the many festive Greek recipes made in celebration of Easter. (Recipes on pages 64 and 66.)

Holiday Meat Pie/ *Kreatopeta*

This is a traditional dish for Carnival and Ascension Day (the Thursday forty days after Easter that celebrates Christ's rise into heaven).

Filling ingredients:

2½-lb. leg of lamb, cut into cubes

4½ c. warm water (heated in a saucepan or microwave, not from the tap)

1 c. minced onions

1½ c. chopped celery

1½ c. minced fresh parsley

1 tsp. minced garlic

1 tsp. minced fresh mint or ½ tsp. dried mint

2 c. tomato sauce

½ c. olive oil

1 tsp. salt

½ tsp. pepper

4 eggs

1 c. grated kefalotiri or Parmesan cheese

1 tsp. ground cinnamon

1 c. uncooked white rice

1 tbsp. butter and 1 tbsp. olive oil for greasing pan

1. Place meat in a large covered casserole dish with warm water. Bring to a boil.

2. Add onions, celery, parsley, garlic, mint, tomato sauce, olive oil, salt, and pepper.

3. Cover and cook over low heat for 1 hour.

4. While meat cooks, prepare crust.*

5. While dough is chilling, remove meat mixture from heat.

6. Beat 4 eggs lightly and add grated cheese and cinnamon. Mix well and add to meat mixture. Add rice to mixture.

7. Preheat oven to 400°F.

Crust ingredients:

3½ c. all-purpose flour, sifted

I tsp. salt

3 tbsp. olive oil

I egg

2 to 3 tbsp. warm water (heated in a saucepan or microwave, not from the tap)

The crust can be prepared in a food processor. Combine all the ingredients and process until mixture forms a ball.

1. Put sifted flour, salt, and olive oil into a bowl and mix well with a fork. Add 1 egg and stir. Gradually stir in warm water until dough is well blended. Knead 5 minutes, or until dough is firm. Cover and chill in the refrigerator for at least one hour.

2. Divide chilled dough into two balls and roll each out on a lightly floured surface to ⅛-inch thickness. Make one piece to line a 15×11-inch baking pan with a lip to turn over the top. The other piece should fit the top of the pan.

3. Grease pan with butter and olive oil. Line with larger piece of dough, then pour in meat mixture, spreading evenly. Cover with second crust, turning the lip of the lower crust over. Crimp the edges. Brush lightly with olive oil.

4. Prick crust a few times with a fork. Bake for 45 minutes, or until crust is golden brown. Allow to sit for a few minutes then cut into squares.

Preparation time: 1 hour 30 minutes
Cooking and refrigeration time: 2 hours 45 minutes
Serves 8

Easter Eggs / *Paskalina Avga*

1 package of red dye

½ c. white vinegar

18 room-temperature eggs

olive oil for glazing

1. Dilute the dye powder in vinegar. In a large pot, combine dye mixture and warm water to cover eggs.

2. Bring to a boil. Simmer, stirring occasionally, for 5 minutes. Remove pot from heat and add eggs.

3. Return to heat and simmer eggs for 45 minutes. Remove eggs and cool slightly. Rub each egg with an oiled cloth to glaze the surface.

Cooking time: 1 hour
Makes 18 eggs

Chocolate Bells / *Sokolates*

1 lb. sweet milk chocolate

1 lb. shelled walnuts or pecans, ground

3 c. powdered sugar

4 tbsp. cream

3 tbsp. rum flavoring

powdered sugar for coating

1. Chop up chocolate into medium-sized pieces. Place in a bowl and set bowl in a shallow pan or dish of hot water to melt the chocolate.

2. When chocolate is smooth, add remaining ingredients. Mix well.

3. Cool slightly. Shape into little bells and roll in powdered sugar.

Cooking time: 35 minutes
Makes 3 dozen

Chocolate bells are usually served at Christmas.

New Year's Bread/ Vasilopeta

Greeks bake a coin inside this bread. At midnight on New Year's Eve, the bread is sliced. According to tradition, the person who gets the slice with the coin will have good luck in the coming year.

1 package active dry yeast

¼ c. warm water

½ c. milk

⅓ c. butter

½ c. sugar

3 eggs

2 tsp. grated orange peel*

1 tsp. grated lemon peel

½ tsp. salt

3 c. unsifted all-purpose flour

1 egg yolk mixed with 1 tbsp. water

blanched almonds

1. Sprinkle yeast into the warm water and stir just enough to blend. Let stand until dissolved.

2. In a small pot, heat milk and butter together until butter melts. Be careful not to let the mixture boil.

3. Empty mixture into a large bowl and add sugar. Cool to lukewarm. Add eggs one at a time and beat with a fork or whisk until smooth. Add yeast. Mix in orange peel, lemon peel, and salt.

4. Gradually add 3 c. of flour, beating on low with an electric mixer for 5 minutes.

5. Place dough on a lightly floured board and knead until smooth and no longer sticky (about 5 to 10 minutes). If necessary, knead in additional flour.

6. Place dough in a large greased bowl and grease the top of the dough lightly with melted butter. Cover with plastic wrap. Let rise in a warm place until dough has doubled in size (about 1¼ hours).

7. Put risen dough on a lightly floured board and knead lightly. If you want, put a washed silver coin in the dough. Shape into a round cake about 9 inches in diameter.

8. Place the dough on a greased baking sheet. Cover and let rise until doubled (about 40 minutes).

9. Preheat oven to 325°F.

10. Brush egg yolk mixture evenly over the loaf. Arrange almonds on top forming the numerals of the coming year. Bake 40 minutes, or until golden brown. Serve warm.

Preparation time: 1¼ hours
Cooking and rising time: 2¾ hours
Makes 1 large loaf

*Use a potato peeler or a zester to gently remove peel in small strips from the lemon and orange. Chop or mince the peel with a knife for even smaller pieces.

Index

About the Author

Lynne W. Villios, a native of St. Charles, Minnesota, graduated from St. Olaf College in Northfield, Minnesota, with a degree in political science. Later she graduated from Vanderbilt University Law School in Tennessee.

Villios learned Greek cooking from her husband's relatives. His grandparents came to the United States from Macedonia before World War I and settled in New York. Villios is an accomplished cook and often makes Greek meals for her friends and family. In addition to cooking, Villios enjoys reading, traveling, and collecting antiques.

Acknowledgements
The photographs in this book are reproduced courtesy of: © Robert Fried, pp. 2–3, 11, 13; Louiseann and Walter Pietrowicz/September 8th Stock, pp. 4 (both), 5 (right), 16, 30, 32, 37, 38, 43, 46, 53, 54, 57, 58, 62, 67; Robert L. and Diane Wolfe, p. 5 (left), 6, 49; © Blaine Harrington, pp. 10, 26.

Cover photos: © Louiseann and Walter Pietrowicz/September 8th Stock.

The illustrations on pp. 7, 17, 27, 31, 33, 35, 36, 39, 41, 42, 44, 47, 48, 50, 51, 55, 56, 59, 61, 63, 65, and 69 and the map on p. 8 are by Tim Seeley.